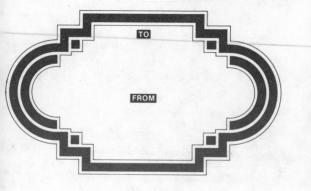

TO

FROM

"I am resolved to be
as wide open toward people
and their need,
as I am toward God.

"Windows open outward
as well as upward."

"I have not tried to pray
in the sense of talking to God,
but I have let God do the talking
with my tongue or in my inner life
when my tongue was silent.

"It has been as simple as
opening and closing
a swinging door."

F.C.L.

Open Windows, Swinging Doors

Personal Diary of
Dr. Frank C. Laubach

G/L REGAL REFLECTIONS

A Division of G/L Publications
Glendale, California, U.S.A.

Cover design by David Koechel
Cover photo by Lucien Aigner

Author's photo by Laubach Literacy, Inc.
Photos on pages 4 and 37 by H. Armstrong Roberts
Photos on pages 15, 22 and 48 Ewing Galloway

Regal Reflection books:
  Words to Live By, Nelson
  Promises to Live By, Wilkerson
  Psalms to Live By, Taylor/Reid
  Proverbs to Live By, Taylor/Reid
  Love to Live By, Sala
  New Life to Live, Munger
  Thoughts for All Seasons, Mears
  Commandments and Promises of Jesus Christ, Wilkerson
  If I Should Wake Before I Die, Ogilvie
  Jesus—Man of His Word, Munger
  Sacred Cows Make Good Hamburgers, Hefley
  Guide to Ecclesiastical Birdwatching, Koopman
  Reach for Life, Ortlund

Second Printing, 1975

Published by
Regal Books Division, G/L Publications
Glendale, California 91209

ISBN 0-8307-0313-6
Library of Congress Catalog Card No. 74-16960
Previously published under the title *Letters by a Modern Mystic*

Foreword

My father, Frank C. Laubach, and mother, the former Effa Seely, both from the town of Benton, Pennsylvania were married in 1912.

Together they chose the island of Mindanao in the southern Philippines for their field of foreign service as Congregationalist missionaries.

In 1915, at a farewell service in the Harvard Church of Brookline, Massachusetts, just before they left for Mindanao, Dad testified, "If I were in a battle and with no orders from my captain, I would be a coward if I fought where we were winning; I would be a man if I fought where our ranks were thin and we were losing the battle. We *are* in a battle for Jesus Christ, to conquer the world, and the ranks are thinnest and the battle hottest in the Orient. So we are going where we are needed most."

Mother and Dad arrived in the Philippines that same year and, though they reached Mindanao and visited lovely Lake Lanao nestled half a mile above the sea, they did not remain in Lanao Province. The situation there was tense, as the government was having trouble with Mindanao's fiercely independent Maranaws, a Muslim people famous for fighting Christians and *conquistadores* alike ever since Magellan set foot on the Philippines in 1521.

The military authorities there felt the presence of neophyte Christian missionaries among the Maranaws at that time would only further compound problems for the government. So my parents settled instead at Cayagan on the northern coast of Mindanao, where they helped start the first congregation of the United Evangelical Church in that city. Then my dad went to

Manila for about ten years to teach in the Union Theological Seminary. There I was born and had my early schooling.

Dad's eyes and prayers were constantly focused on Mindanao, and finally, in 1929, the opportunity came for him to return to the Maranaws, leaving my mother and me behind for a year or so. His first year alone among the Maranaws drove him closer to Christ.

"I had a personal experience of Christ in Mindanao, Philippine Islands," Dad said, "which left me sure that He not only lives, but lives in my heart. When He entered my heart, He brought to me a tender compassion for the multitudes which has been the driving power of my life."

My father's first home there in Lanao was a little summer cottage built on a military reservation at the foot of Signal Hill. He lived there alone, and his only other companions in the immediate area were the local superintendent of schools, the principal of the high school and the captain of the Philippine

constabulary. These men were, in Dad's words, "three fine men—and all of them, like myself, lonesome. While they drowned their loneliness in whiskey, I drowned mine in religion. Every evening at five when the other Americans were at MacSmith's store for their evening comforter, I would climb Signal Hill, back of my cottage, with no one but my black dog Tip, and talk to God and the sunset.

"The first month in Lanao was the hardest of my life. One evening I was sitting on Signal Hill looking over the province that had me beaten. Tip had his nose up under my arm trying to lick the tears off my cheeks. My lips began to move and it seemed to me that God was speaking.

" 'My Child,' my lips said, 'you have failed because you do not really love these Maranaws. You feel superior to them because you are white. If you can forget you are an American and think only how I love them, they will respond.'

"I answered back to the sunset, 'God, I don't know whether You spoke to me through my lips, but if

5

You did, it was the truth. I hate myself. My plans have all gone to pieces. Drive me out of myself and come and take possession of me and think Thy thoughts in my mind.'

"In that terrible, wonderful hour on Signal Hill I became color-blind. Ever since, I have been partial to tan, the more tan the better! Every missionary goes through some such experience as that—or comes home defeated.

"After that night on Signal Hill, when God killed my racial prejudice and made me color-blind, it seemed as though He worked miracles at every turn."

My father continued to meet God nightly on Signal Hill, and God continued to work in and through him enabling Him and his new Maranaw friends to create an entirely new concept of man helping his fellowman through literacy—"each one teach one." Since then much has been written on this worldwide movement, notably by my father himself in *Forty Years with the Silent Billion,* (Fleming H. Revell, 1970).*

But in this little volume you have

in your hands, my father wrote the
words that God filled his heart with
each night up there on Signal Hill.
Dad then wrote letters to his father,
Dr. John Brittain Laubach, a dentist
back home in Benton, and
grandfather sent the letters to the
weekly Benton *Argus,* which
published them faithfully for many
years.

A missionary in Egypt, Miss
Constance Padwick, subscribed to
Dad's hometown newspaper just to
read his letters. The diary on the
following pages consists of those
letters Miss Padwick found most
meaningful to her during the years
1930–32. These words, revealed to
my father by God on Signal Hill,
have already been a blessing to
countless numbers. I trust they will
be a blessing to you, too.

Robert S. Laubach

Robert S. Laubach
Syracuse, New York
1974

*Quoted here by permission of Fleming H. Revell
Company, Old Tappan, New Jersey 07675

1930

January 3
Looking Ahead

To be able to look backward and
say, "This, *this* had been the finest
year of my life"—that is glorious!

But anticipation! To be able to
look ahead and say, "The present
year can and *shall* be better"—that is
more glorious!

If we said such things about our
achievements, we would be
consummate egoists. But we are
speaking of God's kindness, and we
speak truly. We are only being
grateful.

I feel, as I look back over the year,
that it would have been impossible to
have held much more without

breaking with sheer joy. It was the lonesomest year, in some ways the hardest year, of my life, but the more gloriously full of voices from heaven.

Open Windows

I have done nothing but open windows—God has done all the rest. There have been few if any conspicuous achievements. But there has been a succession of marvelous experiences of the friendship of God.

The year closed very beautifully. The young men and girls of Silliman were gathered for a watchnight service, and we were resolving new high resolves until nearly twelve o'clock.

As for me I resolved that I would succeed better this year with my experiment of filling every minute full of the thought of God than I succeeded last year. And I added another resolve—to be wide open toward people and their need, as I am toward God. Windows open outward as well as upward! And especially windows open downward where people need most!

January 20
My First and Last Duty

Living in the atmosphere of Islam is proving—thus far—a tremendous spiritual stimulus. I have no more intention of giving up Christianity and becoming a Muslim than I had twenty years ago, but I find myself richer for the Islamic experience of God.

Islam stresses the *will* of God. It is supreme. And submission is the first and last duty of man.

Submission is exactly what I have been needing in my Christian life. Although I have been a minister and a missionary for fifteen years, I have not lived all day, every day, in minute-by-minute effort to follow the will of God.

Listening to the Inner Voice

Two years ago a profound dissatisfaction led me to begin trying to line up my actions with the will of God about every fifteen minutes or every half hour. But this year I have started out trying to live all my

waking moments in conscious
listening to the inner voice, asking
without ceasing, "What, Father, do
You desire said? What, Father, do
You desire done this minute?"

It is clear that this is exactly what
Jesus was doing all day, every day.
But it is what few of His followers
have been doing since.

January 26
Exploring New Land

I am here exploring two lands
which for me are new. One of them
is within my own soul; the other is in
the soul of the Maranaws.

For the past few days I have been
experimenting in a more complete
surrender than ever before. I am
taking by deliberate act of will,
enough time from each hour to give
God much thought.

Yesterday and today I have made
a new adventure, which is not easy to
express. I am feeling God in each
movement, by an act of will—willing
that He shall direct these fingers that
now strike this typewriter—willing

that He shall pour through my steps as I walk—willing that He shall direct my words as I speak and my very jaws as I eat!

Utterly Free

You will object to this intense introspection. Do not try it, unless you feel dissatisfied with your own relationship with God, but at least allow me to realize all the leadership of God I can. I am disgusted with the pettiness and futility of my unled self.

If the way out is not more perfect slavery to God then what is the way out? Paul speaks of our liberty in Christ; I am trying to be utterly free from everybody, free from my own self, but completely enslaved to the will of God every moment of this day.

Two Burning Passions

We used to sing a song in the church in Benton, (Pennsylvania) which I liked, but which I never really practiced until now. It runs:

"Moment by moment
  I'm kept in His love;
Moment by moment
  I've life from above;
Looking to Jesus
  till glory doth shine;
Moment by moment,
  O Lord, I am Thine."

—D. W. Whittle

It is exactly that "moment by moment," every waking moment, surrender, responsiveness, obedience, sensitiveness, pliability, "lost in His love," that I now have the mind-bent to explore with all my might. It means two burning passions: First, to be like Jesus. Second, to respond to God as a violin responds to the bow of the master.

A Veil over Our Souls

In defense of my opening my soul and laying it bare to the public gaze in this fashion, I may say that it seems to me that we really seldom do anybody much good excepting as we share the deepest experiences of our

13

souls in this way. It is not the fashion to tell your inmost thoughts, but there are many wrong fashions, and concealment of the best in us is wrong.

I disapprove of the usual practice of talking "small talk" whenever we meet, and holding a veil over our souls. If we are so impoverished that we have nothing to reveal but small talk, then we need to struggle for more richness of soul.

As for me I am convinced that this spiritual pilgrimage which I am making is infinitely worthwhile, the most important thing I know of to talk about. And talk I shall while there is anybody to listen. And I hunger—O how I hunger! for others to tell me their soul adventures.

Let the Glory Shine

Outside the window, as I completed the last page, has been one of the most splendorous sunsets I have every seen. And these words came singing through my soul, "Looking to Jesus till glory doth shine!" Glory had been shining all

across the sky until everything was crimson.

Is not this marvelous sky a parable! Open your soul and entertain the glory of God and after a while that glory will be reflected in the world about you and in the very clouds above your head.

January 29
Cooperation with God

I feel simply carried along each hour, doing my part in a plan which is far beyond myself. This sense of cooperation with God in little things is what so astonishes me, for I never have felt it this way before. I need something, and turn around to find it waiting for me. I must work, to be sure, but there is God working along with me. To know this gives a sense of security and assurance for the future which is also new to my life.

I seem to have to make sure of only one thing now, and every other thing "takes care of itself," or I prefer to say what is more true, God takes care of all the rest. My part is

*to live this hour in continuous inner
conversation with God and in perfect
responsiveness to His will. To make
this hour gloriously rich.* This seems
to be all I need think about.

March 1
Unseen Hands

The sense of being led by an
unseen hand which takes mine, while
another hand reaches ahead and
prepares the way, grows upon me
daily. I do not need to strain at all to
find opportunity. It piles in upon me
as waves roll over the beach, and yet
there is time to do something about
each opportunity.

My Mind Set upon God

Perhaps a man who has been an
ordained minister since 1914 ought to
be ashamed to confess that he never
before felt the joy of complete
hourly, minute by minute—now what
shall I call it?—more than surrender.
I had that before. More than
listening to God. I tried that before.

I cannot find the word that will mean to you or to me what I am now experiencing. It is a will act. I compel my mind to open straight out toward God. I wait and listen with determined sensitiveness.

I fix my attention there, and sometimes it requires a long time early in the morning to attain that mental state. I determine not to get out of bed until that mind set, that concentration upon God, is settled. It also requires determination to keep it there, for I feel as though the words and thoughts of others near me were constantly exerting a drag backward or sidewise.

But for the most part recently I have not lost sight of this purpose for long and have soon come back to it. After a while, perhaps, it will become a habit and the sense of effort will grow less.

In Harmony with the Music

I bear witness that people outside are treating me differently. Obstacles which I once would have regarded as insurmountable are melting away like

a mirage. People are becoming
friendly who suspected or neglected
me. I feel, I *feel* like one who has
had his violin out of tune with the
orchestra and at last is in harmony
with the music of the universe.

Eternal and Undefeatable

As for me, I never lived, I was half
dead, I was a rotting tree, until I
reached the place where I wholly,
with utter honesty, resolved and then
re-resolved that I *would* find God's
will, and I *would* do that will though
every fiber in me said no, and I
would win the battle in my thoughts.

It was as though some deep
artesian well had been struck in my
soul or souls and strength came forth.
I do not claim success even for a day
yet, in my mind; not complete
success all day, but some days are
close to success, and every day is
tingling with the joy of a glorious
discovery.

That thing is eternal. That thing is
undefeatable. You and I shall soon
blow away from our bodies. Money,

praise, poverty, opposition, these make no difference, for they will all alike be forgotten in a thousand years, but this spirit which comes to a mind set upon continuous surrender, this spirit is timeless life.

March 9
Let Us Look for God

For the first time in my life I know what I must do here in lonesome Lanao. I know why God left this aching void; it's for Himself to fill. Off on this mountain I must do three things:

1. I must pursue this voyage of discovery in quest of God's will. I *must* because the world needs me to do it.

2. I must plunge into mighty experiments in intercessory prayer, to test my hypothesis that God needs my help to do His will for others, and that my prayer releases His power. I *must* be His channel, for the world needs me.

3. I must confront these Maranaws with a divine love which will speak

Christ to them though I never use
His name. They must see God in me,
and I *must* see God in them. Not to
change the name of their religion,
but to take their hand and say,
"Come, let us look for God."

A few days ago as we came on the
priests, they were praying, in one
boat with thirty-five Maranaws.
Many of them called to me to join.
So I held out my hands and prayed
with them, and as earnestly as any of
them.

One of them said, "He is Islam."
And I replied, "A friend of Islam."

Wrapped in God

My teacher, Dato Pambaya, told
me this week that a good Muslim
ought to utter the sacred word for
God every time he begins to do
anything, to sleep, or walk, or work,
or even turn around. A good Muslim
would fill his life with God. I fear
there are few good Muslims.

But so would a real Christlike
Christian speak to God every time he
did anything—and I fear there are
few good Christians.

What right then have I or any
other person to come here and
change the name of these people
from Muslim to Christian, unless I
lead them to a life fuller of God than
they have now? Clearly, clearly, my
job here is not to go to the town
plaza and make proselytes; it is to
live wrapped in God, trembling to
His thoughts, burning with His
passion. And, my loved one, that is
the best gift you can give to your
own town.

As Rich as God

The most wonderful discovery that
has ever come to me is that I do not
have to wait until some future time
for the glorious hour. I need not sing,
"Oh, that will be glory for me—" and
wait for any grave. *This hour* can be
heaven. *Any* hour for *any* body can
be as rich as God!

God's Experiments

Do you not see that God is trying
experiments with human lives? That
is why there are so many of them.

He has one billion seven hundred million experiments going around the world at this moment.

And His question is, "How far will this man and that woman allow Me to carry this hour? It can be as wonderful as any hour that any human being has ever lived. For I who am reaching out toward divine sons have not become satisfied yet.

"How fully can you surrender and not be afraid?"

This Sunday afternoon at three o'clock He was asking it of us all. I do not know what the rest of you said, but as for me I answered:

"Fill my mind with Thy mind to the last crevice. Catch me up in Thine arms and make this hour as terribly glorious as any human being ever lived, if Thou wilt.

"And, God, I scarce see how one could live if his heart held more than mine has had from Thee these past two hours."

Will they last? Ah, that is the question I must not ask. I shall just live this hour on until it is full, then step into the next hour. Neither tomorrow matters, nor yesterday.

Every *now* is an eternity if it is full of God.

But how "practical" is this for the average man? It seems to me now that yonder plowman could be like Calixto Sanidad, when he was a lonesome and mistreated plowboy, "with my eyes on the furrow, and my hands on the lines, but my thoughts on God." The carpenter could be as full of God as was Christ when He drove nails.

The millions at looms and lathes could make the hours glorious. Some hour spent by some night watchman might be the most glorious ever lived on earth.

A Sacrifice That Hurts

God is not through yet. He is breaking through and I think the poor have less callousness for Him to overcome as a rule than have the rich.

On the other hand the rich man has the wonderful opportunity of paying a sacrifice which will cut his heart almost out. If he seeks the place where his wealth is needed most, then throws all he has into that cause and then throws himself into the cause with his money, as Jesus asked the rich young ruler to do, his money will at that moment be transmuted into the golden threads of heaven. Maybe there is another way, but to me there seems only a blank wall for wealthy men save through the doorway I have entered, a sacrifice that hurts and hurts and—behind Calvary, God!

March 15
Grasping God

How infinitely richer this direct firsthand grasping of God Himself is, than the old method which I used and recommended for years, the reading of endless devotional books. Almost it seems to me now that the very Bible cannot be read as a substitute for meeting God soul to soul and face to face.

By Suffering

And yet, how was this new closeness achieved? Ah, I know now

that it was by cutting the very heart
of my heart and by suffering.
Somebody was telling me this week
that nobody can make a violin speak
the last depths of human longing
until that soul has been made tender
by some great anguish. I do not say
it is the only way to the heart of
God, but I must witness that it has
opened an inner shrine for me which
I never entered before.

March 23
Thinking God's Thoughts

You and you and you and I *do*
experience fine fresh contact with
God sometimes, and do carry out His
will sometimes. One question now to
be put to the test is this: Can we
have that contact with God all the
time? All the time awake, fall asleep
in His arms, and awaken in His
presence. Can we attain that? Can we
do His will all the time? Can we
think His thoughts all the time?

Or are there periods when
business, and pleasures, and crowding
companions must necessarily push

God out of our thoughts? "Of course, that is self-evident. If one thinks of God all the time, he will never get anything else done."

So I thought too, until now, but I am changing my view. We can keep two things in mind at once. Indeed we cannot keep one thing in mind more than half a second. Mind is a flowing something. It oscillates. Concentration is merely the continuous return to the same problem from a million angles.

We do not think of one thing. We always think of the relationship of at least two things, and more often of three or more things simultaneously. So my problem is this: Can I bring God back in my mind-flow every few seconds so that God shall always be in my mind as an afterimage, shall always be one of the elements in every concept and percept?

I choose to make the rest of my life an experiment in answering this question.

Oneness with God

Someone may be saying that this

introspection and this struggle to achieve God-consciousness is abnormal and perilous. But if our religious premises are correct at all then this oneness with God is the *most* normal condition one can have. It is what made Christ, Christ. It is what St. Augustine meant when he said, "Thou hast made us for Thyself, and our souls are restless until they find their rest in Thee."

I do not invite anybody else to follow this arduous path. I wish many might. We need to know so much which one man alone cannot answer. For example:

"Can a laboring man successfully attain this continuous surrender to God? Can a man working at a machine pray for people all day long, talk with God all day long, and at the same time do his task efficiently?"

"Can a merchant do business, can an accountant keep books, ceaselessly surrendered to God?"

"Can a mother wash dishes, care for the babies, continuously talking to God?"

"Can a politician keep in a state of

continuous contact with God, and not lose the following of the crowds?"

"Can little children be taught to talk and listen to God inwardly all day long, and what is the effect upon them?"

Briefly, is this a thing which the entire human race might conceivably aspire to achieve? Do we really mean what we say when we repeat "the highest end of man is to find God and to do His will" all the time?

April 18
Friendship with God

I have tasted a thrill in fellowship with God which has made anything discordant with God disgusting. This afternoon the possession of God has caught me up with such sheer joy that I thought I never had known anything like it. God was so close and so amazingly lovely that I felt like melting all over with a strange blissful contentment. Having had this experience, which comes to me now several times a week, the thrill of filth repels me, for I know its power to drag me from God. And after an hour of close friendship with God my soul feels clean as new fallen snow.

April 19
A Soul's Struggle

This *conscious,* incessant submission to God has proven extremely difficult, and I have surrendered for the past few days. And today and yesterday I saw evidences of the result. In an effort to be witty I have said biting things which have hurt the feelings of others, and I have been short and impatient. I tremble, for I have told at least one of these men of this experiment, and he will think this is the result. It is very dangerous to tell people, and yet, I must tell and I *must* start over *now* and succeed. This philosophy that *one can begin all over instantly at any moment,* is proving of great help.

If this record of a soul struggle to find God is to be complete it must not omit the story of difficulty and failure. I have not succeeded very

well so far. I have undertaken
something which at my age at least,
is hard, harder than I had
anticipated. But I resolve not to give
up the effort.

Yet strain does not seem to do
good. At this moment I feel
something "let go" inside, and lo,
God is here! It is a heart-melting
"here-ness," a lovely whispering of
father to child, and the reason I did
not have it before, was because I
failed to let go.

And back of that failure there
was something else. A crowd of
people arrived who, when they are in
a crowd, wish to talk or think
nothing of religion. I fear I have not
wanted some of them to think me
religious for fear I might cease to be
interesting.

The Other Idol

Fellowship with God is something
one dare not cover, for it smothers to
death. It is like a tender infant or a
delicate little plant; for a long
nurturing is the price of having it,
while it vanishes in a second of time,

the very moment indeed one's eye
ceases to be "single."

One cannot worship God and
Mammon for the reason that God
slips out and is gone as soon as we
try to seat some other unworthy
affection beside Him. The other idol
stays and God vanishes. Not because
God is "a jealous God" but because
sincerity and insincerity are
contradictions and cannot both exist
at the same time in the same place.

April 22
Wide Open and Wide Awake

This afternoon as I look at the
people teeming about me, and then
think of God's point of view, I feel
that we are yet to become what the
spiritual giants have been and more
than many of them were. Here the
selection favors those who keep
themselves wide open toward God
and wide awake.

That waiting, eager attitude ought to
give God the chance He needs. I am
finding every day that the best of the
five or six ways in which I try to

keep contact with God is for me to
*wait for His thoughts, to ask Him to
speak.*

May 14
God's Presence

Oh, this thing of keeping in
constant touch with God, of making
him the object of my thought and
the companion of my conversations,
is the most amazing thing I ever ran
across. *It is working.* Now I *like*
God's presence so much that when
for a half hour or so He slips out of
mind—as He does many times a
day—I feel as though I had deserted
Him, and as though I had lost
something very precious in my life.

May 24
God's Poetry

You must hear of this sacred
evening. The day had been rich but
strenuous, so I climbed Signal Hill
back of my house talking and
listening to God all the way up, all

the way back, all the lovely half hour on the top.

And God talked back! I let my tongue go loose and from it there flowed poetry far more beautiful than any I ever composed. It flowed without pausing and without ever a failing syllable for a half hour. I listened astonished and full of joy and gratitude.

"Why," someone may ask, "did God waste His poetry on you alone, when you could not carry it home?"

You will have to ask God that question. I only know He did and I am happy in the memory.

Sunshine Every Day

Below me, as I sat on Signal Hill, lay the rice fields. And as I looked across them, I heard my tongue saying aloud, "Child, just as the rice needs the sunshine every day, and could not grow if it had sun only once a week or one hour a day, so you need Me all day of every day. People over all the world are withering because they are open toward God only rarely. Every waking minute is not too much."

The "Individuality" of God

A few months ago I was trying to write a chapter on the "discovering of God." Now that I have discovered Him I find that it is a continuous discovery. Every day is rich with new aspects of Him and His working. As one makes new discoveries about his friends by being with them, so one discovers the "individuality" of God if one entertains Him continuously.

One thing I have seen this week is that God loves beauty. Everything He makes is lovely. The clouds, the tumbling river, the waving lake, the soaring eagle, the slender blade of grass, the whispering of the wind, the fluttering butterfly, this graceful transparent nameless child of the lake which clings to my window for an hour and vanishes for ever. Beautiful craft of God!

And I know that He makes my thought-life beautiful when I am open all the day to Him. If I throw these mind-windows apart and say,

"God, what shall we think of now?"
He answers always in some graceful,
tender dream.

And I know that God is
love-hungry, for He is constantly
pointing me to some dull, dead soul
which He has never reached and
wistfully urges me to help Him reach
that stolid, tight-shut mind. Oh, God,
how I long to help you with these
Maranaws. And with these
Americans! And with these
Filipinos!

All day I see souls dead to God
look sadly out of hungry eyes. I want
them to know my discovery! That
any minute can be paradise, that any
place can be heaven! That any man
can have God!

Things Are Happening

As I analyze myself I find several
things happening to me as a result of
these two months of strenuous effort
to keep God in mind every minute.
This concentration upon God is
strenuous, but everything else has
ceased to be so. I think more clearly,
I forget less frequently. Things which

I did with a strain before, I now do easily and with no effort whatever.

I worry about nothing, and lose no sleep. I walk on air a good part of the time. Even the mirror reveals a new light in my eyes and face. I no longer feel in a hurry about anything. Everything goes right. Each minute I meet calmly as though it were not important.

Nothing can go wrong excepting one thing. That is that God *may slip from my mind* if I do not keep on my guard. If He is there, the universe is with me. My task is simple and clear.

And I witness to the way in which the world reacts. Take Lanao and the Maranaws for illustration. Their responsiveness is to me a continuous source of amazement. I do nothing that I can see excepting to pray for them, and to walk among them thinking of God. They know I am a Protestant. Yet two of the leading Moslem priests have gone around the province telling everybody that I would help the people to know God.

June 1
One New Lesson

Inwardly this has been a very uneven week. As a whole my end of the experiment has been failure for most of the week.

But the week with its failures and successes has taught me one new lesson. It is this: "I must talk about God, or I cannot keep Him in my mind. I must give Him away in order to have Him."

That is the law of the spirit world. What one gives one has, what one keeps to oneself one loses.

Do you suppose that through all eternity the price we will need to pay for keeping God will be that we must endlessly be giving Him away?

June 3
God Works a Change

I am not succeeding to keep God in my mind very many hours of the day, and from the point of view of experiment number one I should have to record a pretty high percentage of failure. But the other experiment—what happens when I do succeed—is so successful that it makes up for the failure of number one. God does work a change. The moment I turn to Him it is like turning on an electric current which I feel through my whole being.

I find also that the effort to keep God in my mind does something to my mind which every mind needs to have done to it. I am given something difficult enough to keep my mind with a keen edge. It is a constant temptation to allow the mind to grow old and lose its edge.

I require the very mental discipline which this constant effort affords. So my answer to my two questions to date would be

1. "Can it be done all the time?" Hardly.

2. "Does the effort help?" Tremendously. Nothing I have ever found proves such a tonic to mind and body.

Sacred Palaces

Are you building sacred palaces

for yourself? I meant to write "places" to be sure, but I think I shall leave the word "palaces" for that is what any house becomes when it is sacred. The most important discovery of my whole life is that one can take a little rough cabin and transform it into a palace just by flooding it with thoughts of God.

So in this sense one man after the other builds his own heaven or his hell. It does not matter where one is, one can at once *begin to build heaven,* by thoughts which one thinks while in that place. . . . I have learned the secret of heaven building—anywhere.

No Longer a Stranger

Ah, God, what a new nearness this brings for Thee and me, to realize that Thou alone canst understand me, for Thou alone knowest all! Thou art no longer a stranger, God! Thou art the only being in the universe who is not partly a stranger! I invite others inside but they cannot come all the way. Thou art all the way inside with me—*here*—and every time I forget and push Thee out,

Thou art eager to return!

Ah, God, I mean to struggle
tonight and tomorrow as never
before, *not once* to dismiss Thee. For
when I lose Thee for an hour I lose
and the world loses more than we
can know. The thing Thou wouldst
do can only be done when Thou hast
full swing *all the time.*

June 15
God-intoxicated

I walk out in the street full of
Maranaws, and if my soul is as full
of God as it sometimes is, I see what
happens as I look into their eyes and
pray for them. No man need try to
persuade me that God does not reach
them, for I see the thing happen, and
now I know that every person we
ever meet is God's opportunity, if
only, if only we were not so much of
the time shut off from God.

I saw a little of that marvelous pull
that Jesus had as He walked along
the road day after day,
"God-intoxicated" and radiant with

the endless communion of His soul
with God.

June 22
A Swinging Door

I have just returned from a walk
alone, a walk so wonderful that I feel
like reducing it to a universal rule,
that all people ought to take a walk
every evening all alone where they
can talk aloud without being heard
by anyone, and that during this
entire walk they all ought to talk
with God, allowing Him to use their
tongues to talk back—and letting God
do most of the talking.

For this seems to be the very thing
for which I have been feeling all
these weeks. But this day has been
a different day from any other of
my life, for I have not tried to pray
in the sense of talking to God but I
have let God do the talking with
my tongue or in my inner life when
my tongue was silent. It has been as
simple as opening and closing
a swinging door. And without any
of the old strain the whole day

passed beautifully with God saying
wonderful things to me.

July 2
Contact with God

I have written in this letter what
my tongue said as I let it speak, not
because I wish to recommend any of
it as prophetic, but simply because I
think it may prove helpful to those
who have been dissatisfied with
their own contact with God and
who may find this a helpful practice
in making contacts with
God.

I am well aware of the probability
of criticism because it is
"mysticism"—as though any man
could be a believer in Jesus without
believing in "mysticism"!—and
because many people think that the
days of direct contact with God, or at
least words from God, stopped with
the closing of the New Testament.
But then what a stupid world
this would be if one never did
anything different for fear
of criticism!

July 9
Readier Than Ever

If asked my chief difficulty in meeting these Maranaws, I should have to reply, "No chief difficulty excepting to keep ready spiritually." And I wonder whether here is not the only serious difficulty anywhere. This year I am readier than I have ever been before, and perhaps this is why other people seem readier also.

August 21
All This Wreckage

So many of the people here, and everywhere, seem to have more cramped lives and hopeless minds even than I have. I have been trying to teach a boy to read this afternoon, but his mind seems to be like pouring water into a mosquito net. He could not pronounce "i" without forgetting "a." What a tragedy to live in the world he lives in.

I felt a warm love for the boy, and he felt it, for his eyes were moist as he told me he had neither father nor mother. At times when one looks out upon life all one sees are wrecks, and in upon life, too—wrecks! Ah, God, what is all this wreckage for?

I sat leaning upon my typewriter for a long while after that sentence, for a voice began to talk to me. "The wreckage is the birth pangs of love." And when I wanted to put my arm around that dirty, cross-eyed orphan Maranaw with his stupid brain, I was proving just that.

Not Duties, but Sins

As I sit over in that old building day after day patiently toiling with one man or boy to teach him the alphabet, and so hold him to a larger world, I often wonder whether this work is becoming to a man of my age. But when that same man fondly runs his fingers through my hair and looks his love while he says *Mapia baba*—"good uncle"—I know that a little love is created. If this entire universe is a desperate attempt of love to incarnate itself, then "important duties" which keep us from helping little people are not duties

but sins—or am I all the while
trying to justify my own failure?

I suppose that this self-pity on this
page is an excellent illustration of
our littleness. When I feel like
blaming God, then at that moment I
show the real ugliness of my
selfishness—for I know perfectly well
that I would be quite complacent
about all the innumerable creatures
below man, about all the
innumerable creatures who are barely
man, about all the innumerable
creatures who are robbed of their
manhood by other selfish creatures
like myself, and I would not blame
God for all these if I had all I
wanted.

A prison or a dungeon makes no
difference if one is with God. We
preach and profess that as true, and
it is true, but upon my word I do not
see many people who seem to have
experienced it.

September 2
High Days and Low Days

Tip and I and God were together

49

tonight on Signal Hill. Oh, God, let
me put on paper the glory that was
there. The sunset was not more
beautiful than at other times, but
God said more in it.

There were black clouds which
swiftly turned crimson and pale
yellow. Now those black clouds are
shooting out their fiery tongues
through the darkness. Far off in the
middle of the lake a long, perfect
waterspout stood like a colossal pillar
from the clouds to the splashing
water. Above my head those black,
angry clouds turned into glorious
gold, from the hidden sun.

But it was not this that made the
evening wonderful. God was
speaking.

Three Moral Demands

I patted Tip's head as he
nestled up under my arm, and told
him:

"We are two tiny insects in the
midst of this terrifying universe. I
know a little more than you do, you
nice, black dog, but not much more.
Compared with that gigantic Being

who wheels these awful spheres of fire through the sky I am as near nothing as you are.

"I know as little about God as you know about me, perhaps ten thousand times less. And perhaps you are wiser than I, for you are contented to be patted on the head and to hunt for fleas, while I am impatient to break loose into the universe.

"I thought, Tip, when I was younger, that Kant was wrong when he said the three greatest moral demands are God, freedom and immortality; but now I believe he was incredibly right. My soul at forty-six demands immortality as much as it demands God. And it demands freedom from this prison we call the world and the flesh as much as it demands immortality."

Prison and Paint Box

Then out of the skies there came a silent voice, "Your black clouds give the sun its chance. It is surprise, it is escape from darkness to light that

makes life so rich. Your prison
is also your paint box from which
all the beauty you know is
pouring.

"And here you have the privilege
of opening eyes to see beauty, which
otherwise they would not see. It is
selfish of you to desire to escape,
until you can take humanity with
you. You are not Christlike until you
demand that even after you die, your
soul shall stay and help others come
through to the larger life.

"I almost fear that my nightly
visions, much as I love to give them
to you, are making you more selfish,
more hungry to get, less eager to
give. The most beautiful thing in the
universe for you is Lanao stretching
around this lake at your feet, for it
contains the beauty of immense need.
You must awaken hunger there, for
until they hunger they cannot be
fed."

Oh, tonight I so hunger to be able
to tell what else happened. But that
other thing was all emotion, a
painfully sweet stretching forth of
arms skyward to receive and
Lanao-ward to give.

Our search for God through narrow straits has brought a sudden revelation, like an explorer who has just come out upon a limitless sea. It is not any particularly new idea, but a new feeling. Today God seems to me to be just behind everything. I feel Him there. He is just under my hand, just under the typewriter, just behind this desk, just inside the file, just inside the camera.

One of these Maranaw fairy tales has the fairies standing behind every rock looking at the hero. That is how I feel about God today. Of course this is only a way of symbolizing the truth that God is invisible and that He is everywhere.

For a lonesome man there is something infinitely *homey* and comforting in feeling God so close, so *everywhere*! Nowhere one turns is away from friendship, for God is smiling there.

It is difficult to convey to another the *joy* of having broken into the new sea of realizing God's

53

"here-ness." Just the privilege of fellowship with God is infinitely more than any *thing* that God can give. When He gives Himself He is giving more than anything else in the universe.

September 22
The Presence of God

It is as much our duty to live in the beauty of the presence of God on some mount of transfiguration until we become white with Christ, as it is for us to go down to men where they grope and grovel and groan, and lift them to new life.

After all the deepest truth is that the Christlike life is glorious, undefeatably glorious. There is no defeat unless one loses God, and then all is defeat though it be housed in castles and buried in fortunes.

October 7
Joy in Endless Giving

It is that spirit of greed which

Jesus said God hated more than any other. It is so diametrically opposite to the Spirit of God. For God forever lavishes His gifts upon the good and bad alike, and finds all His joy in endless giving.

You see, I feel deeply about us all. Beside Jesus the whole lot of us are so contemptible. I do not see how God stomachs us at all. But God is like Jesus and, like Jesus, He will not give up until we, too, are like Jesus.

October 12
Perpetual Peace

Worries have faded away like ugly clouds and my soul rests in the sunshine of perpetual peace. I can lie down anywhere in this universe bathed around by my own Father's Spirit. The very universe has come to seem so *homey*! I know only a little more about it than before, but that little is all! It is vibrant with the electric ecstasy of God! I know what it means to be "God-intoxicated."

Unusual Love

How fine of these Maranaw boys to come and lean on one's knee, or run their fingers through one's hair—or rub the bald spots and ask why they are so! They know that we love them.

Less than a year ago we were writing about "the most difficult place under the American flag, if not in the world!" No, New York City is the most difficult place in the world, for in New York they demand ability, unusual ability, while here in Lanao, they demand only love—unusual love.

And the love of God may be had for the receiving.

October 15
The Great Stirrer Up

Has God ever struck you as the *great stirrer up*? One thing He seems to have determined is that we shall not fall asleep. We make or discover paradises for ourselves, and these paradises begin to lull us into sleepy satisfaction. Then God comes to take us by the shoulders and give us a thorough awakening.

And God knows we need it. If our destiny is to grow on and on and on, into some far more beautiful creatures than we are now, with more of the ideals of Christ, then we need to have our shells broken quite frequently so that we can grow.

A Better Way

My confidence that this earth is but a brief school grows into certainty as my fellowship with God grows more tender. As a discipline this world is admirable.

Jesus said, "Fix not your desire upon this earth, but lay up all the desires you can for a fuller life, which begins within you now, and is endless."

Many people seek other escapes. Some in prodigious work, some in reckless play, some in drugs, some in insanity—for insanity is but an escape from pitiless, crushing failure. But I wish to tell all the world that needs a better way, that God on Signal Hill

57

satisfies, and sends through me a glow of glory which makes me *sure* that His is the true pathway.

December 6
The Cross and Beauty

Sometimes one feels that there is a discord between the cross and beauty. But there really cannot be, for God is found best through those two doorways. This grey-blue rolling water tinged with whitecaps, hemmed with distant green hills and crowned with colored clouds and baby-blue sky, reveals God's love of beauty.

But there is in the universe a higher kind of beauty. It is the beauty of sacrifice, of giving up for others, of suffering for others. A woman has not reached her highest beauty until she lays down her ease and chooses pain for bearing and nursing her child. A man has not found his highest beauty until his brow is tinged with care for some cause he loves more than himself.

The beauty of sacrifice is the final word in beauty.

1931

February 6
The Only Doorway

Tonight, lonesome and half ill with a cold, I am learning from experience that there is a deep peace that grows out of illness and loneliness and a sense of failure. It is "the peace of God that passeth all understanding," except the understanding of one who possesses it.

God cannot get close when everything is delightful. He seems to need these darker hours, these emptyhearted hours to mean the most to people. You and I have known that over the coffin. We have known it when we parted and our

hearts were sore. We have known it
when we lay in bed helpless.

Is this a deep truth in the very
heart of nature? We sing,

"Nearer, my God, to Thee, nearer
to Thee!
E'en though it be a cross that
lifteth me."

Is the cross the only doorway to
the very heart of God?

February 10
What We Are Now

This afternoon I climbed my way
to the top of Signal Hill weighted
with a sense of remorse. Everything
wrong that I have done in twenty
years came back and made me feel
like a dreadful sinner.

I told God about it, but do not
intend to write any confessions here.
We are so eager to judge people by
their past, and it is not fair. We are
what we are now, not an hour ago;
and what we are planning, not what
we are vainly trying to forget.

As I stood on the top very much
inclined to let the tears break out of

my eyes, my tongue stopped talking
to God and began talking from God
to me.

"Ah, little child, I have hurt you
tonight, and now I feel sorry with
you. All you have confessed is true,
but I love you still. I love you for
coming here and telling me about it.
I love you for hungering after me. I
love you for being willing to be
better. That is all I ask of people.

"Ah, I have wanted to do so much
for you as soon as you would allow
it. Now, with a sore and lonesome
heart you are ready."

This Need of Pain

And into my heart there stole
another new love for God I never
knew so strongly before. I felt like
saying:

"God, I thank Thee that Jesus
showed us that Thou art burning,
yearning, eager to do more for us
than Thou canst.

"Thou art like those plowmen who
must break the soil and tear it apart
before seeds will grow. Thou hast
plowed my heart tonight until it is

61

tender and ready for something to grow. I thank Thee, God, I thank Thee, because I could not have felt Thine healing hand if the pain had not been so acute.

"God, how can we reconcile this need of pain with our effort to abolish all misery?"

The answer was convincing to me:

"If you abolish the physical suffering of the world, there will still be disappointed love, yearnings which cannot be satisfied, which will leave hearts bleeding even as they do today. Mansions have as many burning hearts as do poor houses. The things which drag men down to grossness and incessant selfishness must be wiped out. Then hearts will become sore over infinitely larger things than selfish needs. They will learn to bleed for a world with the heart of Jesus."

There will be more suffering than today, for only love knows how to suffer divinely. But the meanness of suffering for one's own selfish disappointments will be gone, and we will see a magnificence and sublimity in suffering that will make us glad.

February 25
You Learn by Doing

As I lay on the warm earth on Signal Hill last night I asked God the question:

"Why is it that Thou dost allow us on this earth to do nearly all the talking? Why do we not always hear Thy voice, since Thou art so much wiser than we are?"

Instantly back came the answer:

"When you are teaching the Maranaws to read, your art is to say as little as you can and leave them to say as much as they will. That is why I leave you to do and say as much as you can, while I say little. You learn by doing, even when you make mistakes and correct them.

"You are to be sons and daughters of God, and now you are taking the first feeble steps of infants. Every step you take alone is infinitely more important than you now imagine, because the thing I am preparing you for exceeds all your imagination. So the talking you do to Me is essential.

"The talking others do to you

when they are trying to talk up to your expectations is more important than the talks you give to them. This is the best way to act: Talk a great deal to Me. Let others talk a great deal to you, appreciating everything fine they say and neglecting their mistakes."

March 3
Carry Glory into Business

Oh, if we *only* let God have His *full* chance, He will break our hearts with the glory of His revelation until we ache with bliss. And that is how I feel this morning after two hours of wonderful thinking with God.

And now on this "mount of transfiguration" I do not want ever to leave. I want to keep this lovely aching heart forever. But that would not be Christlike. I must now carry all I can of Him across the river to the Maranaw school. There are figures and there are salaries to be considered for it is the end of the month. How much of this glory can one carry into business?

April 5
On Trial with Jesus

We see ourselves on trial with Jesus. He could walk into the jaws of death to do His blessed work for others. He could dare to speak out against wrong and take the consequences. He could receive floggings; could allow men to spit in His face; could endure the agony of thorns in His head; could be taunted, without a word in reply or even a thought of anger; could think of His mother, while writhing on the cross; could cry, "Father, forgive them, for they know not what they do."

I have read books which said that these words were evidently imaginary, for nobody *could* say anything when suffering the excruciating torture of hanging by nails. But Jesus was such an "impossible" person more than once in His life. This scene fits into His whole character. True, nobody else can think of others when suffering like that, but Jesus was better than the rest of us. Tragedy, magnificent horror! The best man who ever lived dying because He was too good to run away.

That would have driven humanity more deeply into despair. They might or might not have remembered Jesus. I think they would have tried to forget Him. For humanity wants to believe that God is good, and the Crucifixion portrays God forsaking the finest example of loyalty we can find. God was betraying His staunchest defender. That cross alone is horrible. The God who would allow the drama to stop there would be a monster or dead, "My God, why . . . ?"

Unless We Have Easter

So we cannot believe in a good God unless we have Easter. It is a difficult story to believe, because we have had nothing else quite like it before or since. But it is only the difficulty of believing the unprecedented.

On the other hand to doubt it is far more difficult.

I must either rule out the whole story of the life of Jesus or else rule out any intelligence or heart from the universe. And if I do that my troubles are far more than intellectual—they become moral. I cannot actually sacrifice myself for others, at least not to death, for, noble as it may sound, it is folly. The act of Jesus becomes not only rash and useless but misleading to the rest of mankind.

I Choose Christ

"How is it proved? It isn't proved, you fool! It can't be proved. How can you prove a victory before it's won? How can you prove a man who leads to be your leader worth following unless you follow to the death, and out beyond mere death, which is not anything but Satan's lie upon eternal life. . . . And you? You want to argue. Well, I won't. It's a choice, and I choose Christ."

—Studdert Kennedy.

That last sentence is the crux of the whole matter; it is a choice, and while choosing Christ brings mystery, rejecting Him brings despair.

September 28
Using God as My Glasses

The fashion today is to place God in court and give Him a trial. We have had such a lust for "debunking" every good and useful man in history that even God cannot escape. It is one of the unfortunate by-products of the quest for truth, plus an unlovely hunger in humanity for scandal. It is a species of jealousy. We dislike to believe that anybody else is quite as good as we are, not even God.

As for me, I choose to stop following this current, to stop posing as the judge of the universe. I choose another road for myself. I choose to look at people through God, using God as my glasses, colored with His love for them.

No Longer Lonesome

Last year, as you know, I decided to *try* to keep God in mind all the time. That was rather easy for a lonesome man in a strange land. It has always been easier for the shepherds, and the monks, and the

anchorites than for people
surrounded by crowds.

But today it is an altogether
different thing. I am no longer
lonesome. The hours of the day from
dawn to bedtime are spent in the
presence of others. Either this new
situation will crowd God out or I
must take Him into it all.

I must learn a continuous silent
conversation of heart to heart with
God while looking into other eyes
and listening to other voices. If I
decide to do this it is far more
difficult than the thing I was doing
before. Yet if this experiment is to
have any value for busy people it
must be worked under exactly these
conditions of high pressure and
throngs of people.

There is only one way to do it.
God must share my thoughts of
Maranaw grammar, and Maranaw
epics, and type, and teaching people
to read, and talking over the latest
excitement with my family as we
read the newspapers. So, I am
resolved to let nothing, *nothing,* stop
me from this effort save sheer fatigue
that stops all thought.

One need not tell God *everything* about the people for whom one prays. Holding them one by one steadily before the mind and willing that God may have His will with them is the best, for God knows better than we do what our friends need, yet our prayer releases His power, we know not how.

Respond to the Limit

I cannot get God by holding Him off at arm's length like a photograph, but by leaning forward intently as one would respond to one's lover. Love so insatiable as the love of God can never be satisfied until we respond to the limit. Nor will He be satisfied until His aching arms receive my neighbors, too, and all the surging multitudes of the world, all of us together responding to Him and to one another.

September 28
Heaven on Earth

When one has struck some

wonderful blessing that all mankind has a right to know about, no custom or false modesty should prevent him from telling it, even though it may mean the baring of his soul to the public gaze.

I have found such a way of life. Just to pray inwardly for everybody one meets, and to keep on all day without stopping, even when doing other work of every kind. This simple practice requires only a gentle pressure of the will, not more than a person can exert easily. It grows easier as the habit becomes fixed.

Yet it transforms life into heaven. Everybody takes on a new richness, and all the world seems tinted with glory. I do not of course know what others think of me, but the joy which I have within cannot be described. If there never were any other reward than that, it would more than justify the practice to me.

Today I have noticed that when I forget other people I become fatigued rather quickly. When I am reminded of my purpose and start again holding people, seen and unseen, before God, a new exhilaration

comes to me, and all the fatigue
vanishes.

October 11
Friendship Demands Growth

Knowing God better and better is
an achievement of friendship. "When
two persons fall in love there may be
such a strong feeling of fellowship,
such a delight in the friend's
presence, that one may lose oneself
in the deepening discovery of another
person." The self and the person
loved become equally real.

There are, therefore, three
questions which we may ask:

First, "Do you believe in God?"

That is not getting very far. "The
devils believe and tremble."

Second, "Are you acquainted with
God?"

We are acquainted with people
with whom we have had some
business dealings.

Third, "Is God your friend?" In
other words, "Do you love God?"

It is this third stage that is really
vital. How is it to be achieved?

Precisely as any friendship is achieved: by doing things together. The depth and intensity of the friendship will depend upon variety and extent of the things we do and enjoy together.

Will the friendship be constant? That again depends upon the permanence of our common interests, and upon whether or not our interests grow into ever widening circles, so that we do not stagnate.

The highest friendship demands growth. "It must be progressive as life itself is progressive." Friends must walk together; they cannot long stand still together, for that means death to friendship and life.

Friendship with God is the friendship of child with parent. As an ideal son grows daily into closer relationship with his father, so we may grow into closer love with God by widening into His interests, and thinking His thoughts and sharing His enterprises.

Helping God

Far more than any other device of

God to create love was the cross where the *lovingest* person the world has known hangs loving through all His pain. That cross has become the symbol of religion and of love for a third of the world because it touches the deepest depths of human love.

All I have said is mere words, until one sets out helping God right wrongs, helping God help the helpless, loving and talking it over with God. Then there comes a great sense of the closeup, warm, intimate heart of reality. God simply creeps in and you *know* He is here in your heart. He has become your friend by working along with you.

So if anybody were to ask me how to find God I should say at once, hunt out the deepest need you can find and forget all about your own comfort while you try to meet that need. Talk to God about it, and—He will be there. You will know it.

1932

January 2
Hold God by the Hand

In school a teacher lays out work for his pupils. I resolve to accept each situation of this year as God's layout for that hour, and never to lament that it is a very commonplace or disappointing task. One can pour something divine into every situation.

One of the mental characteristics against which I have rebelled most is the frequency of my "blank spells" when I cannot think of anything worth writing, and sometimes cannot remember names. Henceforth I resolve to regard these as God's signal that I am to stop and listen.

Sometimes you want to talk to your son, and sometimes you want to hold him tight in silence. God is that way with us; He wants to hold still with us in silence.

Here is something we can share with all the people in the world. They cannot all be brilliant or rich or beautiful. They cannot all even dream beautiful dreams like God gives some of us. They cannot all enjoy music. Their hearts do not all burn with love.

But everybody can learn to hold God by the hand and rest. And when God is ready to speak the fresh thoughts of heaven will flow in like a crystal spring. Everybody rests at the end of the day. What a world gain if everybody could rest in the waiting arms of the Father and listen until He whispers.